UPPER MISSISSIPPI RIVER STEAMBOATING
DAYS STORIES

The Virginia, the first steamboat on the Upper Mississippi, passed up the river on her way to Fort Snelling, Minnesota, in 1823   With the settlement of the Old Northwest the number of steamboats multiplied year after year. Nine out of every ten boats we e built on the Ohio river   They were of two types—stern and side wheel   The largest measured up to 300 feet in length   They often carried as many as 500 passengers   They cost from \$20,000 to \$40,000   George B Merrick, historian, compiled a list of about 1500 boats which were in use on the Upper River between 1823 and 1900   These were packets, raft boats and ferry boats   The loss of boats up to 1897 by snags, fire, ice, collisions, explosions and other causes numbered 295.   Other boats were worn out and dismantled   Steamboating began to decline in about 1870 with the building of railroads to St Paul and other important river towns

For these stories we are indebted to George B Merrick and Harry G Dye , noted old time rivermen   To them this booklet is dedicated.

STEAMBOAT RACES

Steamboat racing was one of the pleasures of the old time river captains, who took great pride in the appearance and speed of their boats   "One of the fastest steamboats on the Upper Mississippi was the swift ʻ Key City," the champion of the Minnesota Packet Company fleet. She was never beaten by any steamboat outside of her own line, and by but one boat in her line—the peerless "Grey Eagle "   She shone at all times like a star of the first magnitude   She was a very pretty boat to look at, beautifully proportioned and very serviceable, a river greyhound

Her captain, James Worden, was a real sport and always ready to accommodate any boat with a race and at any old time   Hank Whitney was her very efficient chief engineer. He always had plenty of rosin on hand and had no objection to "perching a nigger or two on her safety valve "   She never suffered a single defeat (1857-66)   Captain Worden had a broom with a brush about three feet wide and with a long handle by which it could be firmly affixed to the roof of the pilot house   This broom he offered to any boat that would take it away from the "Key City"   He at the same time offered to wager any sum on the result of her racing.   Her reputation was known the length of the Upper River.

Of course every captain who had a fast boat sought the first opportunity to test Captain Worden's claims The "White Cloud," a fast side-wheeler, tried conclusions with the 'Key City" and was beaten The "Northener", a really fast boat, had a race with her through Lake St Croix This was a river classic The race began at St Paul and ended at Pres- cott. Here the "Key City" hoisted her broom Ned West was the pilot of the winning boat, "as fine a pilot as ever turn- ed a wheel "

In one of her following races the "Key City", leaving St. Paul heavily laden with freight, beat the "Keokuk" to Lake City by over two miles Then she beat her to Reads Landing by about one and one-half miles At Wabasha her com- petitor was one mile behind the "Key City" The "Key City" made business landings at Alma, Minnieska, Fountain City, Winona and Trempealeau, thus consuming over an hours time and yet she was only one mile behind her opponent when the "Keokuk" reached La Crosse The supremecy of the "Key City" was unquestioned

The "Key City" was loafing along upper Lake Pepin, towing a heavy barge, when she met the "Messenger", a big and fast Lower River side-wheel steamboat The latter blew her whistle, a challenge for a race That was enough for Captain Worden He put some men aboard the barge and set her adrift His firemen began sifting in rosin with the cordwood, and, it is presumed, hung a grate-bar on the safety valve It did not take the "Key City" long to strike her gait The chimneys of both boats were soon red-hot The "Key City" soon overhauled and passed the "Messenger" Running far enough ahead of her to make such a proceeding safe she ran across the bow of her rival, and circling back returned to her barge

Other fast and powerful steamboats, among them the "Tish- n.ongo", "Tigress" and "Resolute" tried to wrest her laurels from the "Key City", but all had to take the wash of her stern

The fast run of the "Grey Eagle" in 1858 between Dunleith (East Dubuque) and St Paul was 24 hours and 3 minutes, with 21 landings The "Key City's" time for the same run was 24 hours and 29 minutes with 13 landings. She was very nearly as fast as the "Grey Eagle", the queen of the Upper River The "Key City" was the grandest boat in the Minnesota Packet Company line. Stories of her triumphs are still told whereever old rivermen gather.

THE CALLIOPE ON THE DENMARK

The 'Denmark', a side-wheel packet of the St Louis line (1856-62), was the first passenger boat on the Upper River to sport a steam piano, or calliope This was in position on her hurricane deck This "music-maker" was added to her equipment by her captain, Robert C. Gray, "as a persuader of custom" from the traveling public of her day. Among the rivermen "opinions differed as to the direction her passengers were persuaded to take—on board or overboard. It was confidently averred that the same passenger never booked himself for a passage on the "Denmark" a second time " Several deluded travelers are said to have ended a more or less miserable existence by jumping overboard enroute However, to the general public, not "fed-up" on her music, her arrival and departure from the levee of the river towns was a real musical treat The performer on the calliope was a "real artist and could play popular songs, national airs and well-known hymns with equal facility and enjoyment." "As soon as the "Denmark" rounded the bend of the river below St. Paul the calliope would start to play That was the signal for everybody, and by the time the boat arrived, the levee was crowded with people."

The "Clarion", a small stern-wheel steamboat, had "a whistle in keeping with her name, but out of all proportion to her size It was said that her builders at Monongahela, Pennsylvania, took the whistle and then built a boat under it. It was so large that it made her top-heavy They said that the engineer always had to shut off his engines when the pilot began blowing for a landing " So strong and loud was her blast that a Dutchman in one of the river towns once fell out of the second story window of a hotel when he heard her "wissle" and permanently injured his person.

CAPTAIN STEPHEN B. HANKS

Most famous of the raftsmen of the Upper Mississippi was
Captain Stephen B. Hanks He was born at Hodgenville,
Kentucky, in 1821. and was a cousin of Abraham Lincoln In
1841. when living at Albany, Illinois, Stephen, a healthy and
strong young man, left home for the pine woods of the St
Croix valley. Here he found employment as a lumberjack
cutting timber and helping to drive the logs to the saw mill at
St Croix Falls Here he helped to raft and float the lumber
to St Louis "In 1844 he made his first trip as pi'ot of a log
raft that floated all the way down the Mississippi from Stillwater at the head of Lake St Croix to St Louis "* This was
an undertaking which probably no other riverman could have
successfully accomplished in that early day of log rafting
The distance, as the river channel ran, was "a good. long
seven hundred miles.'* After ten years of rafting Captain
Hanks became a steamboat pilot From that time on until
the year 1892 he stood at the wheel of the fine boats of four
different large packet lines His was a life or rare achievement
He was ninety-six years old when he died in 1917 He was
a Christian gentleman, and "he was held in high esteem by
all who knew him " (Walter A Blair, A Raft Pilot's Log)

THE GREEN TREE HOTEL

On the river front at Le Claire there stands a grand o'd
elm tree, dear to the hearts of many old time rivermen Its
semi-globular crown of foliage has to-day a spread of nearly
one hundred feet and its huge trunk is over twelve feet in cir-
cumference This monarch among trees is located at an Iowa
Mississippi River town which enjoyed great prominence in old
steamboating and rafting days as the home of the skilful
rapids pilots and of other steamboatmen of note Its landing
was a stopping place of many great and small steamboats on
their way down river. Here they secured pilots to take their
boats over the Rock Island rapids.

In the shade and shelter of this great tree, known as the
"green tree hotel", many riverman, temporarily out of em-

ployment, once found a retreat All were welcome there In this riverside "tavern" there was no landlord to greet, no register to sign, and there were no lodging bills to pay Put your hat anywhere and stay as long as you like! A man might spread his blanket here or there, or, if he had none, use his coat or shirt for a pillow On many a summer night lodgers were plenty, river tales were told and river songs were sung. Here a steamboat or raft boat captain might hire a cook, a fireman, deckhands or a raft crew. Much has been written about this famous tree This sylvan hostelry was known to steamboatmen and raftsmen the whole length of the Upper River This historic landmark still stands and is cared for by the citizens of this river town

TOO MUCH PEPPER

Commodore William F. Davidson of the old White Collar Line of Mississippi River steamboats was a very pious man It was his custom to assemble the members of his crew on deck on Sunday mornings and to there hold a prayer meeting On such occasions he always offered the prayer himself. One of these prayers he once concluded, according to a river tale, with the following words.

"And Oh Lord bless the poor Give to every poor family a Barrel of Pork,—a Barrel of Flour,—a Barrel of Sugar,—a Barrel of Salt,—a Barrel of Pepper" Then, hesitating for a moment, he added.—'Oh h--l no—that's too much Pepper!"·

There were other river captains who were well known for their piety One of these was a resident of La Crosse, a fine upright man, yet this steamboatman was also known to be able to swear harder than almost any riverman of the Upper Mississippi when occasion seemed to require it. In the back-yard of his home there was a fine apple tree The boys of the neighborhood annoyed the good captain very much by stealing its fruit. On one occasion he caught a number of them in the act. Then he let forth such a stream of finished profanity that the young thieves were almost scared to death One of them has since stated that he will never until his dying day forget the continuous explosion of swear words which the old officer emitted on this occasion.

ROLLING STONE COLONY

Land sharks operated along the banks of the Upper Mississippi as they did elsewhere in the Middle West, promoting paper townsites and relieveing their victims of their money "One of the boldest-faced of these swindlers was the so-called Rolling Stone colony In the spring of 1852, some three or four hundred people, chiefly from New York city, came to seek their purchased lands in Rolling Stone They brought with them beautiful maps and birds-eye views of the place, showing a lecture hall, library and academy Each colonist was to have a house lot in the town and a farm in the neighboring country None had ever had any farming experience. Boarding steamers at Galena, they expected to be put off at the Rolling Stone levee, for the views represented large houses, a hotel, a big warehouse and a fine dock But the steamboat officers had never heard of such a place Careful investigation. however, seemed to locate the site three miles above Wabasha. on land belonging to the Sioux Indians As they insisted on landing they were put off at the log cab n of the only white man within ten miles They made sod houses for themselves. or dug shelter burrows in the river banks. Sickness came, many died during the summer and autumn, and when winter set in the place was abandoned The people suffered severely, and the story of Rolling Stone makes a sad chapter in the early history of Minnesota "

ONCE WAS ENOUGH

On June 14, 1872, the "D. A McDonald", a famous boat owned by the Van Sant Navigation Company, on her up-river trip. was near North Mc Gregor. when her boilers exploded, killing or drowning eighteen out of twenty-seven men on board—one of the most disasterous explosions ever recorded on the Upper Mississippi Among those killed was Captain Martin Several of the survivors of that disaster had most remarkable experiences. "W. N. Pierce, of Rock Island, an engineer, was on board the steamboat as a guest He was lying in his berth over the boilers, reading The blast sent him high up in the air, ahead of the boilers and without getting scalded by any of the steam He had a thrilling experience, going up pretty well toward the zenith, turning a complete somersault or two, going down to the foundations of the earth under water, coming to the surface and swimming ashore, all within the space of a very few minutes But, boys,' said Mr. Pierce, 'once is enough I don't want any more boiler explosions in mine'"

One of the crew, Charley Johnson, also lying in his berth, was blown through the door, or window of his room On his mattress he fell in the river about forty feet from the boat. Here he caught a big oar, and straddling this he paddled ashore He had not suffered a scratch. At McGregor he found a dugout and started down river to his home at Le Claire. News of the explosion and of his death had already reached his home town. When he got there some boys, who were swimming at the levee, saw him paddling toward the shore, they fled for home, not even stopping for their clothes When he passed through the town, he cleared the streets wherever he went, the people believing him to be a ghost and not a flesh and blood visitor His family had mourned him for dead, and inscribed the date of his demise in the family Bible.

THE UNLUCKY ALEX MITCHELL

There is a superstition among rivermen that certain steamboats are "hoodooed", and can never be successfully operated Such a boat was the "Alex Mitchell", a passenger packet (1870-81). "She was thought to be the unluckiest boat ever on the Upper River If there was anything in the river or over the river, she hit it When there were no snags to encounter she would bump an island or climb a tree Hers was a chapter of accidents To enumerate all of the scrapes she got into would fill a book."

"In 1871 she hit the island at the foot of Coon Slough doing considerable damage to herself In 1872 a cyclone tried conclusions with her The mate, who was sitting by her big bell, was blown a quarter of a mile, lighting on the shore without serious injury The pilot was blown out of the pilot house This was believed by some to have occurred because Captain Laughton had permitted the members of a German excursion to dance on her deck on Sunday, contrary to the laws of God and of Commodore William F Davidson, one of the owners of the steamboat line to which she belonged In July 1878 the "Mitchell" was snagged and sunk at Oquawka, Illinois She was raised In November of the same year she hit another snag and was sunk, this time at the mouth of the Des Moines River In December 1876 she was damaged $5000 by ice at St. Louis, and, in 1879, by the bridge at Hastings. In 1881 she was dismantled at La Crosse, after a "glorious" river career

The "Alex Mitchell" was valued at $30,000 when new being built at La Crosse in 1870 She belonged at first to the Northwestern Line, then to the Keokuk Line, and, finally to Commodore Davidson's St Louis and St Paul line, the famous White Collar Line

STRONG MAN OF THE RIVER

Captain Oscar F Knapp, of Osceola, was "the father of steamboating on the St Croix River" First to last he was the owner, builder and captain of a number of different boats Captain Knapp "was a giant, physically, several inches over six feet tall, and weighing over two hundred pounds"

In the fifties and sixties hundreds of lumberjacks rode on his boats on their way to the mills and the pineries Many of these passengers would pay their passage only under compulsion Captain Knapp insisted on their fares He kept his "compulsion" with him all of the time It was always on "tap" and ready for use When one of the "jacks" refused to pay the good Captain signalled the pilot to run as close to a towhead as possible. Then catching the unwilling "jack" by the

scruff of his neck and the slack of his pants, he simply tossed
him ashore. When this action was resented by five or six of
his fellow pirates, the Captain was willing and ready to "lick"
the whole gang. One blow of his fist always settled the big-
gest bully of the lot. At one time or another the Captain
thus "colonized" with "jacks" every big sandbar along the
picturesque St. Croix In spite of his primitive methods of
preserving order Captain Knapp's boats were always popular
with the old time loggers and raftsmen.

TOO MANY BELLS

There were a few captains on the river who seemed to have
a passion for ringing bells George B Merrick tells of a pilot
who had this bell-ringing habit From the pilot house he
would keep the engineer and his second over busy executing
his orders given in this way On one trip the engineer got
so far behind with these orders that after the steamboat had
tied up to the bank at a landing it took him "seven hours and
a half" to catch up with his bells

"CYP." BUISSON

"Cypriane Buisson had been on the river since he was a boy,
most of the time in the rafting trade—for twenty years captain of one boat. "Cyp", as he was generally known on the
river, knew the Mississippi well from St Louis to St Paul,
up-stream, down-stream and crossways by day and night. He
was conceded to be one of the very best raft pilots on the
river. He had plenty of nerve, but no nerves. He never got
flusterd In every kind of dilemma or danger he was as
cool as under ordinary conditions. An old steamboat engineer said that "Cyp" never rang all of the bells at once,
never kicked all of the sash out of the pilot house, and never
swore so that it created a blue fog so thick that he couldn't
see his bow-boat, what-ever the stress might be That was
the river way of saying that he kept cool"

DIAMOND JOE

Among the widely known big men of the old Mississippi
River steamboating days was Joseph Reynolds, "Diamond Jo",
owner of a great majority of the stock of the famous Diamond
Jo Line of steamboats This was in its day a great corpora-
tion, controlling an investment of half a million dollars Its
fleet of freight and passenger steamboats was large and fine

Joseph Reynolds, birthplace was at Fallsburg, New York,
and the date 1841 He received a common school education
When he was seventeen he began buying cattle, sheep and
hogs, peddling the meat in the surrounding country In the
winter he taught school for the meagre wages of $10 a month
and his board Later he and his brother opened a general
store at Rockland, New York Here he married Mary E. Morton. Her father furnished the money for the purchase of a
feed and flour mill Later he became the owner of a tannery
also. Both proved very profitable. After a few years he sold out
and came to Chicago Here, in about 1856, he established a
tannery In the interests of this business he traveled ex-
tensively in Illinois and Wisconsin. In shipping packages of
hides and furs to Chicago he caused them to be marked with
his nickname "Jo" stamped upon a diamond shaped figure To
this "trademark", rather than to the large diamond which he
wore in later years in his shirt front or scarf, the origin of
his nickname is correctly traced Negro roustabouts patched
the seats of their pants with Diamond Jo "trademarks" cut
from wornout bags.

In about 1860 Mr Reynolds disposed of his Chicago business and engaged in the grain trade at Prairie du Chein, then
the terminus of the Milwaukee & Mississippi Railroad. In
order to obtain better shipping facilities than the steamboat
lines would furnish he built in 1862 the steamboat "Lansing"
She carried grain and produce between Lansing and Prairie
du Chien In the winter of 1862-63 he built at Woodman,
Wisconsin, the "Diamond Jo". He also built barges for bulk
grain. In 1868 he began his first operations as a steamboat
line with four boats and Fulton, Illinois, as his headquarters.
Here he had a shipping agreement with the Chicago & North-

western Railroad Here he built and purchased other boats extending the service of his boats to St. Paul. In these years, 1858-74 he handled many million bushels of grain That year the general offices of his line were moved to Dubuque Here, at Eagle Point, he also established a shipyard where many of the best steamboats and raft-boats on the river were built in the next twenty years Captain John Killeen was the very efficient general superintendent of the company In 1880 the company began to pay more attention to the passenger traffic. The passenger packets (1881-86) included the large and beautiful steamboat, "Mary E. Morton", the "Sidney", ' Pittsburg" and "Josephine" In 1883 the line incorporated as the 'Diamond Jo Line of Steamers' Mr Reynolds was its president It continued without change until his death in 1891

"D.amond Jo" Reynolds was respected and loved by his associates and employees He was a very quiet man and had little use for "society " He was well known at many steamboat landings along the river between St Louis and St Paul If one saw a quiet, modest-looking man seated on a box or bale at a steamboat levee, whittling a stick and paying attention only to his own business, that was likely to be "Diamond Jo" Reynolds He amassed a great fortune in the steamboat business

GEORGE BYRON MERRICK

In the years 1854 to 1858 two boys. George and Samuel Merrick 'bunked" in the garret of their father's (L H Merrick & Co) warehouse at the old steamboat landing at Prescott, Wisconsin. 'There were two windows fronting the river and no steamboat ever landed at the levee day or night without two boy spectators carefully noting its distinguishing characteristics " So these lads came to know the steamboats of that day by their shape and size, by their wheels, by the trimmings on their smokestacks, their pilot houses, the colors of their outside blinds and the sounds made by their bells and whistles.

"All of these points and many others, were taken in, and indelibly impressed on their memories, so that if the whistle or bell were again heard, perhaps months afterward, the name

of the boat could be given with almost unfailing accuracy It
was a part of the education of the "levee rats", as the boys
were called. A boy, that could not distinguish by ear alone
a majority of the boats landing at the levee from year to
year, was considered as deficient in education Every boy in
town could tell what craft was coming as soon as she whistled
Every boat had a whistle toned and tuned so that it might
be distinguished from that of any other boat of the same
line The bells, which were always struck as the boat came
into the landing, also differed widely in tone" And thus the
Merrick boys "grew into the very life of the great river as
they grew in years" Soon George was ripe for river adven-
ture He obtained a job as pantry boy on the "Kate Cassell ,
a stern-wheel steamboat, and remained a member of her crew
during the season Of course he was very proud of his job
on this fine boat The next spring he became a "cub" engineer
on another steamboat, the "Fanny Harris'" He learned the
machinery of the boat His next step upward came when he
became "mud clerk", or second clerk, of the steamer The
duties of a second clerk were arduous He assisted and re-
lieved his chief in attending to all of the business of the boat,
writing up delivery books, checking out freight, measuring
wood, and attending to a hundred other duties that fell to his
lot He collected the fares of passengers, assigned rooms, collected freight bills, paid for wood and other supplies. Then,
at last, came the opportunity to learn the duties of a "cub"
pilot from two of the master steamboat pilots of the Upper
River Under their able instruction he learned the channels,
the marks and the intricacies of steering a steamboat The
height of his boyhood ambition to become a pilot was attained Then came the Civil War, and in 1862 George enlisted
and marched away to the front with his regiment, the Thir-
tieth Wisconsin Infantry After the War he entered the em-
ploy of a steamship company in New York. Returning to
Wisconsin he entered the newspaper business, and finally became the auditor of the University of Wisconsin

George B Merrick's interest in the Great River and its history continued until the date of his death, in 1931 He became the recognized historian of the Upper Mississippi River

In 1909 he published a book, "Old Times on the Upper Mississippi", and in later years he contributed many other valuable
articles, papers and monographs in which the history of old
steamboating days on the river is graphically recorded Thus
this man, who in his boyhood had watched from an attic win-
doy of his father's warehouse the big steamboats come and
go, made his mark as an author and historian

THE TIN FISH

On the crest of a high, wooded river bluff at Minnieska there
was for many years a large wooden "fish", supported on the
top of a tall pole This very conspicious sign was known to
all of the steamboatmen and raftsmen plying up or down the
waters of the Mississippi They found it a convenient and
unerring guide-post, as well as a weathervane, as it swung
around on it wooden pivot Adult passengers and children,
who were being transported on the packets and who were
curious about the wooden "fish", often asked questions about
it They were told, in reply by the pilots, mates or members
of the steamboat crew, that the Great River was once as deep
as the height of the bluffs, and that in the recession of the
waters this particular "fish" was left stranded, pinioned to the
top of this tall pole

In recent years this landmark was replaced by a tin fish
(16 feet long) and supported by an iron pole upon which it
turned, its head always pointed in the direction of the wind
It continues to be a landmark of interest to riverfarers

BILLY HENDERSON

Billy Henderson was a well-known fruit man and steamboat bar magnate of the 60's In 1854 or 1855 he owned the
bar on the steamboat "Excelsior" As a side line he peddled
oranges and lemons at the various steamboat land ngs from
St Louis to St Paul He was known the length of the river
as "Billy". Later this was changed to "Old Bill" Henderson
Even in his younger days he was inclined to be severely
economical He generally wore a red or blue flannel shirt

that he had traded in with some returning lumberman for the out-put of his gin-mill Some carping critics said that he wore this style of shirt because it never required washing

As he attained age and wisdom he bought other bars, until finally he owned the "drug stores" on every boat of the Northern Line He put in bartenders whom he hoped that he could trust to make correct returns. But he never did trust them, always complaining that he was being robbed He became wealthy despite his dishonest toddy-mixers

In his later years he had an axiom which he always imparted to his younger friends It was "Never carry any money in your pocket If you have money in your pocket you will spend it If you have no money in your pocket you can't spend any money I never carry any money in my pocket, so I never spend any money". If a newsboy asked him to buy a paper he would draw the boy aside and take particular pains to explain to him why he never carried any money. It was said that when he died he did not take a cent with him—consistent to the last

LILLY PADS

Captain George Tromlye, who was taking a raft boat down river, called his son Charley, whom he was teaching the river, to take his place at the pilot wheel while he himself took a little rest In the middle of the night he arose and went to the pilot house to see how things were going with his son He asked Charley where he thought that he was Charley replied that they were in Crooked Slough, which is near Lynxville. "Crooked Slough your ear!" exclaimed Captain Tromlye, and added, "EVER SEE LILY PADS IN CROOKED SLOUGH??" Charley had run the boat down a dead-end slough. This was in about 1875.

THE YOUNG PILOT

Captain Jerry Turner was the captain and pilot of the steamboat "Pauline", in 1890. Walter Hunter was the other

pilot, Harry G. Dyer, the mate One day Captain Turner
had a felon on his thumb and wanted to leave the boat at his
home town of Canton, Illinois The trouble was that there
was no pilot to spell Mr Hunter while he was away Hunter informed him that there was a man on board who could
steer and called Dyer He took him into the pilot house and
told him to take the wheel Dyer steered while Captain Turner
sat in the rear and criticized

"You turn your wheel too much," said he No answer from
Dyer.

"You turn your wheel too much!" said Captain Turner
again Dyer paid no attention. "YOU TURN YOUR WHEEL
TOO MUCH!" said the Captain in a last attempt to instruct
the pilot. No answer from Dyer. That was all, Captain
Turner arose, slammed the pilot house door behind him and
went away Old pilots always moved the wheel from one
side to the other, young pilots kept the nose of the boat con-
tinually on the mark by moving the wheel just very slightly
from side to side

WRECK OF THE SEA WING

A marine disaster, which occurred on the waters of beautiful Lake Pepin nearly a third of a century ago, will furnish
a topic for conversation in that region for many years to
come The loss of the "Sea Wing", on July 13, 1899, was a
major event in Upper Mississippi Valley steamboating days
history On that date Captain David Wethern, the owner
of this small stern-wheel boat, was conducting an excursion of
some 170 happy residents of Diamond Bluff and Red Wing
to the Minnesota National Guard encampment at Lake City
The excursionists were mostly women and children Not a
few of the women had husbands, brothers and friends among
the soldier boys, and all looked forward with pleasure to an
enjoyable day to be spent in their summer camp.

In the afternoon, while the "Sea Wing" and the covered
barge, which she towed, were moored at the landing at Lake
City, masses of dark clouds were seen to be forming in the
sky As the weather began to look stormy the excursionists

had assembled at the landing All were very enxious to make
a start for home Captain Wethern argued with them He
knew the uncertain temper of Lake Pepin in a storm He
tried in vain to persuade them to remain at Lake City until
it had passed They were so insistent in their demands that
he depart that he finally yielded to their request This was
at about 8 o'clock in the evening The little "Sea Wing", with
her freight of many precious human lives, entered on the
fateful voyage that was to lead to their destruction

She was near Maiden Rock, enroute to Red Wing, when
the storm struck her and the barge She had gone hardly two
miles It struck with the force of a tornado, and the little
craft was soon bowled over like an eggshell "The scene was
a nightmare Before she capsized many persons rushed from
the barge to the boat The barge, cut loose was swept away
down the lake by the heavy gale She finally ran aground
with her passengers safe and sound The scene aboard the
capsizing 'Sea Wing" was terrible Overhead a terrible storm
was in progress Thunder roared, lightening flashed and a
gale, that assumed the proportions of a tornado, made the
waters a perfect hell Men, women and children struggled to
save themselves, but to no avail When the storm subsided
only a handful had been saved, and nearly five score had gone
down to watery graves Among these were the wife and
daughter of Captain Wethern The work of rescue was be-
gun at once All through the night bodies were washed or
brought ashore These were laid in a long row on the beach,
awaiting recognition by relatives and friends Fifty-one
bodies were taken to Red Wing More were recovered later,
until a total of ninety-nine were found This grim tragedy
cast a gloom on lake excursions, and for years afterward there
were no excursions on Lake Pepin" The captain was blamed
for this harrowing disaster, because he left port when his own
judgement told him that he should have remained there

CAPTAIN ROBERT DODDS

This little story was told of Bob Dodds, captain of the raft
boat, "Charlotte Boeckler" At St Louis his crew frequented a

saloon kept by a Mrs Murphy down on the levee. As soon
as his men entered the saloon Mrs Murphy would drive all of
the other patrons away from the bar with the words: 'Get
back from me ba-a-r-r ye paper-collar dudes   Here comes
Bob Dodds and his red-shirted rafters!" And all would go
back in a hurry The patronage of this crew was nearly always good for fifty dollars The 'Charlotte Boeckler" made
regular trips with log and lumber rafts from the Schulenberg
and Boeckler lumber mill at Stillwater to their yard at St
Louis in the years 1881 to 1892

THE PRAYER

The steamboat captain stood on the deck of his boat which
had struck a snag and was sowly sinking. He spoke to the
frightened passengers who were huddled on the main deck
"Is there anyone among you who can pray?" A meek little
man in the crowd stepped forward and replied, "Yes, I can
pray."

"Good", said the captain, "you start praying while the rest
of the passengers put on life preservers We're one short"

THE PROTEM LADY

When business was light on one of the boats the chamber-
maid was ordered to put on her bonnet and best "togs" and
sit on the boiler deck where she could be seen by the crew
of the opposition packet when they met her on the river This
was to show that the boat was carrying all of the passengers
that wished to travel As soon as the other boat had passed
it was back to the washtubs for the protem "lady."

THE ASPARAGUS BOAT

In the fifties a river packet, name unknown. was proceeding
up-stream She was bound for St. Paul and was carrying a
heavy cargo of freight. Among this merchandise were some
packages or bags of asparagus seed, this toothsome vegetable
being then almost unknown in the home gardens of the Upper

River towns When this vessel reached Lake Pepin she struck
a snag which ripped up her botton so badly that she sank in
a comparatively short time What became of her crew no
one knows Presumably, they, or most of them saved their
lives by swimming, or floating to the tree-grown shore The
packages of asparagus seed, which were on her lower deck,
floated ashore Some of this seed later germinated there, and
in the years following asparagus plants were distributed along
the roadside and in the fields near Bogus Creek and elsewhere,
between Pepin and Stockholm To-day, in the asparagus
season, people from Pepin and elsewhere go to this neighborhood to collect his fugitive asparagus Few of them have
heard of the illfated steamboat which is said to be respon-
sible for its presence Asparagus roots from this region have
been planted in gardens in the entire country round. (Local
Myth)

COMMANDEERING THE COAL

Captain George Winans was coming up the Mississippi in
about the year 18/0 with his steamboat, the "Juliana", and
towing a barge loaded with coal. He had delivered a log raft
at St Louis and was returning to Stillwater When he reached a locality just below Burlington he found Captain Ira B.
Short there with his boat the "Mountain Belle" Captain
Short was moving down-river and had got the log raft he was
towing stuck on a sand-bar He was vainly trying to extri-
cate it When Captain Winans stopped to inquire about his
trouble, Captain Short, who was a man of an imperious
nature, said, "George, I'll have to commandeer that barge of
coal!" He feared that his boat would run out of fuel before
he got the raft off the bar His words and his attitude so ir-
ritated Captain Winans that he yelled in reply. "No— you
ain't going to commandeer my barge of coal! And if you
try to do it, —— there will be trouble! I licked the whole
Short family once, and, by G-d, I can do it again if you say
so!"

As boys George and Ira were playmates. George lived in
one river town and Ira in another On one occasion George

gave Ira a licking, and Ira's two brothers entering the fight
he whipped them also   Hence the above reminder

WHAT COULD HE DO

Captain Jerry Webber, when a Mississippi river pilot, was
once being examined by the U S Steamboat Inspectors for
a license In the course of his examination he was asked the
following question — 'Captain what would you do if your
boat was moving along and you suddenly saw a big rock
sticking up out of the water right in front of your boat? You
could not go back."

"By—," said Captain Webber without a moments hesita-
tion, "I'd bust into it." No one could have done otherwise,
the examing officer agreed

Captain Webber could swear harder than any captain on
the Upper river Often he would do this quite unconsciously
He had a woman cook on the boat and sometimes he would
say to her. "Now Mrs. Black just get as far back on the boat
as you can, so you won't hear me I'm going to talk "

GO BACK WHERE YOU WERE

One of the best raft captains of the Upper Mississippi was
Captain William Dobler He was an able, courageous and re-
sourceful steamboatman   He was "one of the best raft pilots
that ever lived and held the record for log raft towing One
year he made eight trips from the rafting works at West New-
ton to the Gem City Lumber Company at Quincy, Illinois, in
64 days' Quincy is 120 miles below Rock Island

One year in making a sharp river turn at Skunk Flats near
Pontussa, Illinois, one end of his raft caught a sand-bar As
soon as George Walker, the other pilot, heard the noise he
jumped out of bed and started upstairs for the pilot house
Captain Dobler saw him coming and said, "Go right back
where you were George I got her into this and — — I'll get
her off." And he reversed and slowly backed the steamboat
off the sand

THE ROUSTABOUT

When a certain steamboat left St Louis she carried a gang of negro roustabouts to load and unload the freight When the boat reached a landing one of the colored hands of this gang could never be found. When the unloading of the freight was accomplished and the boat again on its way, this nigger would appear from somewhere When asked by the mate where he had been he said that he had been asleep When the next landing was reached the darkey would be gone again The mate searched everywhere for him but could not find his hiding place This happened a number of times during the boats journey At last the mate, thoroughly mystified, called the negro before him He promised him that if he would reveal his hiding place he would not require any more work from him until the steamboat reached its destination This being agreed upon, he asked the man, "Now where was your hiding place?"

"Why," answered the grinning black, "I'se been in your baid."